Backyard Sunflower

story and photographs by ELIZABETH KING

DUTTON CHILDREN'S BOOKS · NEW YORK #31098

Library of Congress Cataloging-in-Publication Data
King, Elizabeth.
Backyard sunflower/story and photographs by Elizabeth King.—1st ed.
p.   cm.
Summary: Text and photographs follow the life cycle of a sunflower,
from the time that Samantha plants a seed in her garden to the maturity
of the sunflower and the harvest of its own seeds.
ISBN 0-525-45082-3
1. Sunflowers—Juvenile literature.   [1. Sunflowers.]   I. Title.
SB299.S9K47   1993   635.9′77355—dc20   92-31002   CIP   AC

Published in the United States 1993 by Dutton Children's Books,
a division of Penguin Books USA Inc.
375 Hudson Street, New York, New York 10014

Designed by Amy Berniker
Printed in Hong Kong
First edition
1 3 5 7 9 10 8 6 4 2

For Samantha and Claire, best friends

My deep-felt thanks to members of the Nolet family, which spans three generations—Samantha, Barbara, Michael, Ethel, and Gordon Nolet.

To Don Lilliboe, of Fargo, North Dakota, the editor of *The Sunflower* magazine...a thank-you for your time, knowledge, and oral histories.

To my husband, Dale, for all your support...but more importantly, your rototilling!

To the sunflower kids: Samantha Nolet, Alix and Kaci Taylor, Aaron and Allison Jaeger, and Taylor and Claire Ettema.

Other people who deserve thanks are: Dr. Jerry Miller and Dr. Brady Vick, USDA-ARS, of the Northern Crop Science Laboratory in Fargo, North Dakota; Susan Van Metre, of Dutton Children's Books; Mr. and Mrs. Orland Hellert; Robbie Taylor; Dolores Johnson; Nick Marcarelli, of Home Depot; Constance Hofland, of the National Sunflower Association; Brad Newton, of Red River Commodities, Inc.; Steve Temple, at the University of California at Davis; Becky Purdy, at the Fargo Convention Center; Candy Jaeger; Kathleen Minor; and Bruce Due, of Sigco Research.

Besides all of the other talented and supportive people at Dutton Children's Books, I would especially like to thank my editor, Lucia Monfried, once again, for her unerring taste and direction.

Under the hot August sky, a giant sunflower stands. It is taller than anything growing around it. Bright yellow petals encircle the sunflower's round head, making it look like the shining sun above.

The flower is growing in a backyard garden. It is Samantha's sunflower.

She planted a row of sunflower seeds in the spring.
Carefully, Samantha made a furrow for the seeds in the
garden plot. She measured the distance between each seed
with her sneaker. The sunflowers need lots of room because
they grow to be very large plants!

When the planting was done, Samantha could rest. Then the waiting began. It is hard to wait.

Every day, Samantha inspected her garden. She watered it and looked for a bit of green above the soil.

A week after planting, a seedling pushes its way through the earth covering the seeds.

Sometimes the striped shell of the seed clings to the seedling after it sprouts. But it soon falls off.

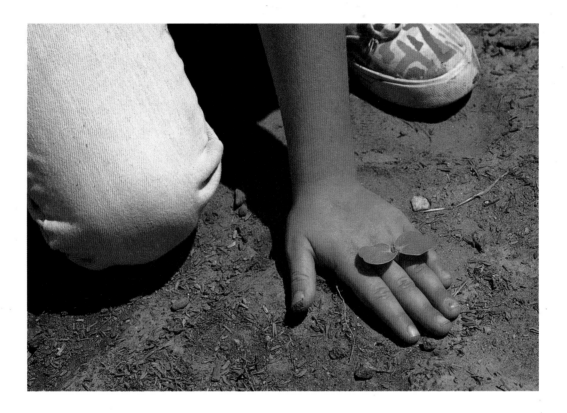

Samantha takes good care of her garden. She visits it every day. In just two weeks the seedling looks like an emerald ring for her finger. Just the right size!

Sunflowers grow one deep taproot into the ground. The taproot is the main root of the plant. It is long and shaped like a tube. It takes the food and water the plant needs from the soil. The food and water are drawn up through the stalk to reach the leaves and, later, the flower on top. The stalk is like a giant straw.

Aboveground, the sunflowers sprout sets of dark green leaves, one above the other. The leaves at the bottom are large. Those at the top of the plant will be smaller. That way the sun can shine on all of the leaves.

With water and sunlight, the plants grow fast. In just a month, they are over two feet tall.

Samantha and her mother examine the big, soft leaves.

The veins in the leaves look like the veins in Samantha's own hand. The plant uses sunlight to make its food. The food for the plant is made in the leaves. The veins in the leaves and stem carry the food to the rest of the plant.

Day after day, the sunflowers stretch skyward. Each morning, the sunflowers face east, toward the rising sun. By evening, the leaves have turned west to face the setting sun. Scientists believe that the growing sunflower plant follows the sun as it crosses the sky so the leaves can get as much light as possible.

The plants have grown large leaves. They make a shady place to hide.

After about six weeks, small tight buds appear in the middle of the plants. The flowers begin with these little buds. Pointed green leaves called bracts surround the buds, protecting them.

As the plant grows taller, the stalk grows thicker. The stalk needs to be strong to support the sunflower's large head when it is full of seeds.

Several more weeks pass. Now the plants are taller than a grown-up person. The buds of the flowers have grown too.

Eight weeks have passed since Samantha planted her seeds.
Now the buds begin to open. Bright yellow petals show
through the green bracts. These petals are called ray petals.

Over the next few days, the ray petals slowly unfold around
the sunflower head like a golden crown.

The bright color attracts bees and other insects to the flowers. The insects land on the sunflower's head, which is made up of hundreds of small flowers called florets.

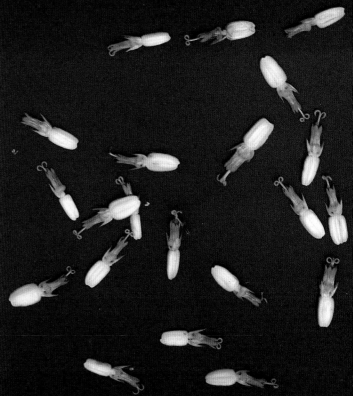

At the base of each floret is a seed kernel. The sunflower has hundreds of them on its head—one for each floret. The picture above right shows some small seed kernels, each attached to a floret.

As they brush against the florets, insects sometimes leave pollen from other florets they visited. Once a floret has been touched with pollen, its seed kernel will begin to grow.

The seed kernel is the inside of the seed. The hull is the outside, the part of the seed that you crack with your teeth when you eat sunflower seeds.

Dazzling in full bloom and as bright as the sun, the plants are full grown. They no longer follow the sun but stand tall facing the east.

Samantha's sunflowers are a type of sunflower grown for food. People and birds love to eat this plant's seeds, which are rich in protein and iron. Sunflowers grown for food are called confectionary sunflowers.

Samantha invites her friends over to see her sunflowers. The plants are so tall the children have to use ladders to reach the heads, where the seeds are growing.

The sunflowers begin to "dry down" in the hot sun. The heat makes the water inside the plant evaporate. The ray petals wither. The weakened stalk bends under the weight of the head, heavy with drying seeds.

The florets dry up and blow away.
    Underneath them nature's perfect design in rows of black
and white can be seen.

Samantha planted a small patch of sunflowers. But farmers in the Midwest grow fields of the plants on big farms. The farmers grow crops of confectionary sunflowers and another kind, called oilseed sunflowers.

The oilseed sunflowers have small black seeds. When the oilseed sunflower seeds are harvested, they are taken to large processing plants, where they are pressed for sunoil. The sunoil is used in salad dressing, margarine, and other foods, and it can even be added to diesel fuel!

One special sunflower smiles in the farmer's field. Children
made its smiling face by brushing away some of the dry florets
with their fingers to make a design.

In Samantha's sunflower patch, it's time to harvest the seeds. She and her friends remove them from the sunflower heads. The children will roast some and eat them for snacks in the coming months. The rest they will save…

to plant in next year's backyard garden.

635.9   King, Elizabeth.   c.1
KIN
         Backyard sunflower.

$13.99   34621000310980

BAKER & TAYLOR